GERARD BEIRNE has pub
collections of poetry, *Digg*
Press, 2016) and *Games of Ch*
was shortlisted for the Kerry (
Danuta Gleed Literary Awar
stories), and the Bord Gáis En   ... ᴅᴏᴏᴋ Awards. He
won the Hennessey New Irish Writer of the Year Award and
was runner-up in the Patrick Kavanagh Poetry Award.

THE DEATH POEMS

GERARD BEIRNE

The Death Poems

Songs, Visions, Meditations

SALT

CROMER

PUBLISHED BY SALT PUBLISHING 2023

2 4 6 8 10 9 7 5 3 1

First published in Great Britain in 2023 by
Salt Publishing Ltd
12 Norwich Road, Cromer, Norfolk NR27 0AX United Kingdom

www.saltpublishing.com

Salt Publishing Limited Reg. No. 5293401

A CIP catalogue record for this book is available from the British Library

ISBN 978 1 78463 273 1 (Paperback edition)

Typeset in Sabon by Salt Publishing

Printed and bound in Great Britain by Clays Ltd, Elcograf S.p.A

For Luke

Contents

SONGS

VISIONS

MEDITATIONS

SONGS

The Song of the Dead-Child Being

In a small cobbled together box of distraught wood under my father's
    weathered arm,
wrapped in white cloth, knocked from side to side with the squall of his
    uneven walk
along the knobbled lanes between the scrabbled hedge, the clinging grass
    and the scattered stones.
The hard to swallow procession he led in fraught fashion in the throbbing
    rain.
The tall evening shadow of him alone amongst the walking dead. No talk,
    just the windswept
breath of the stillborn bereft of the hard wrought pain of the unnamed,
    the shamed depths
of the thrown-upon-us skies, dense and black and warm, crowding the
    worn path of heather
along the cliff's torn edge, the thin veil of the calm sea, the unfledged life
    of the impending storm.
And up ahead, the shallow grave the spade has dug, the small impression I
    have made, the shrug
of earth, the dirt shovelled back and closing in, the stray-sod darkness,
    and the hungry grass.
Trapped in the dismal doings of the day, the ruins of the hardened clay, a
    banished child forever
doomed to carry a candle and wander in the wilds of night with all the
    other baby-lights.
I glimmer outside the graveyard walls, my vanished time measured and
    stalled in flight,
the endless ventures towards the hallowed ground that I approach and yet
    can never enter.

The Song of the Dead Christ
after The Body of the Dead Christ in the Tomb *by Holbein*

Caught between the mutilation of the body and the decomposing flesh,
this thought is mine, my corpse will never rise again. *The ground cracks
and the earth opens to the abyss.* This abomination of my life, the unnameable
death, contemptible in its caesura, laid out on the slab of the mortuary table.
The measure of the tombstone weighs upon me, the low vault separating
outside from in. The sinistra, dark and insolent, cast into shadow by a ray of light
striking underneath, piercing the soles of my feet, the palms of my wasted hands.
My emaciated body, rigid and battered, horribly thin. Abandoned to this hermetic
isolation as if nothing else mattered. Mysterious and inaccessible even to myself.
My grey skin suffused with blood, obscenely bruised, the gangrened flesh green,
swollen with sin. The blank whites of my eyes stare in helpless condemnation.
The terrible anguish, all hope shattered, utterly forsaken. My pale lips open
with insipid prayers that go unanswered, go unspoken. The finger that extends,
pointing without consolation, simply and abjectly stating – this is where it ends.

The Song of the Dying

I sail towards death in a skiff of bronze, gilt oars in my hand,
bring down a sea bird with my sling, revive it in on the strand,

suffer the cauldron on my back, grasp the shank of the silver ladle,
rub cow-dung upon my hair, scoop the bird up in my girdle.

I pour soured milk into the stream where the women wait to bathe me,
brandish my sword at every beast that has risen on wings to slay me.

Carvers carve, cup-bearers pour, for I'll ride the waves of the crimson flood
upon a horse of four green legs, a bridle encrusted in gold and blood,

my bowels fallen at my feet, my stone set up, my grave made.
Let no calf be let to its cow nor the cry of my lament be raised:

'Woe to the land where you come from, I am taken to the sea to drown.'
Lay the strap of your shield upon my arms so I may kill my only son.

The Song of the Blind Heretic Harper

Men beget, Women conceive, Every nostril breathes the air
Dawn comes and their children have gone to their tomb
Harper's Song: Tomb of Neferhotep

Spur-blind or purblind and half mulvadered from a pipe of wine
and two hogsheads of liquor, I weathered the withering roads

on a dim-witted horse led by a half-minded guide into the hobbles
of near-extinction, a scurrilous cur with a harp next his thigh.

Meanly obscene and pregnant with smutty songs and tales, I rode
straight into the mortuary feast professing the harp to all blind children.

Raisins, figs, prunes, and gingerbread in honour of the deceased,
piled high next the priest with his lowly wife by his rapturous side,

while I new-strung my harp and sang my song of the rambunctious dead:
'Damn your soul you humping rascals, Ye excellent nobles and gods

of the graveyard and anyone else that pleases to drink their skinful.'
All who come into being pass on, and young blood mounts to their places.

You built your mansions and you built your tombs with your weed ashes
and your privy purses, your sealing money on all signed leases.

Go burn your whiskey in a wooden bowl with canes of sugar
on the bitter tongs. Scum the seething pot with a skelp of straw.

Eat the entrails of unwashed beasts, unsalted beef, the flesh of swine
and swallow down with unstrained milk the filthy lumps of butter.

Rub incense and sweet oil upon your head, grub garlands of lotus
from your breast, cast behind you your drinking and swearing, the blind

addiction to grotesque lust. I'll squat before you and play my songs.
One says, welcome safe and sound to him who reaches the west.

The Song of the Desiccated Wife

Having agreed upon a price and I in sweet repose, a wife of someone noble
    and high repute,
he lies between my thighs and with his hook extracts my brain through my
    less than perfect nose,

pours oils upon the surface beauty of my skin and within the cavities that
    decompose. Then with a knife
of stone, hand-carved and Ethiopian, traces out my soft and fleshy
    abdomen before slicing it deep-open

to remove the coils of spoiled intestine and rinse me clean with choice palm
    wine, spice that's bruised.
Do not despair: he fills me in again with cassia, cinnamon and myrrh and
    sews me up in sweet repair,

then runs his fingers through my greying hair and dying it with henna,
    restores the colour of my youth.
And in some preservation of the truth, my organs – liver, lungs, intestine,
    stomach – in alabaster jars

are stored, canopics with human headed lids. For forty days he leaves me
    there to air, embalmed
in natron, saltpetre, until later, all dried out and wrapped in linen, he
    plaster-coats me in a resin,

beeswax, pistachio, and bitumen, amulets entrapped within to bring me
    safely home. Then noticing
the creases on my cheeks and eyes and mouth, he fabricates a plaque of
    cartonnage, a mummy mask,

a gilded face attached for me to wear upon my desiccated hide and bone.
    And all too late, professing
his undying love for me alone, accepts his fate and lies beside me upon my
    weak and mortal throne.

The Song of the Bean Chaointe

Who'll rescue me from my wandering life across the fields where there are
   no paths,
the shade of the blackthorn, the chill of the frost, the weight of the cold
   earth upon my back?

Who'll bare my breasts to press my milk, smear me with blood, stretch me
   out on my bier,
unshod and dishevelled, my clothes wrought with hunger, grief snatched
   from my eyes, torn from my hair?

Who'll take my coffin of unseasoned timber, fastened with sailcloth and
   hardened nails
or carry my corpse through remnant ruin, a scattered tomb, 'cross miles
   of place?

Ah, the priest he may beat me, whip prayers from my cracked lips as the
   hailstones hiss on bracken and moss,
pay me off with tobacco, with alms and with fasting, with whiskey and
   salt, exclusion from mass.

But it's myself I am keening, the abominable idolatries, the revel and
   banquet, the excess of lust,
so sing out of season and call up my sad death, the shadows sustained on
   milk and on blood.

I am there in the valley, I am there on the seashore, I am there on the
   mountains, I am down, I am done
with the shrieks and the wailing, the screams and the bawling, long as the
   day is, the night's still to come.

Snow white is my virtue, I am gazed on with rapture, and old age listens
   to the song of my tongue,
keeps my house with the walls sound and turf in my kitchen, my hens to
   the hatching, my butter to churn.

For the silence prevails me, the awful silence, the grim tyrant has taken
  the green stick from the wood.
My birthless sicknesses have no requital, the home wrecker strokes the
  hammer for good.

So lament at my bedside and prolong my agony. If you take me out feet-
  first, I'll jump in my grave.
Each failed rebellion's but a final rehearsal, and if I was faithful, my
  daughters were chaste.

The Song of the Bone-Grubber

Miles I walked out, my fighting days over, before and round back, a bone-
    grubbing man,
where the cabmen chaffed ale or drank porter from pewter, then off to
    their no-beds without measure of time.

The skim-milk skinned bumpkins and swarthy-eyed women with
    mongrel-dog faces and burst-bluchers tongues,
their smocks and their buskins, their corduroy breeches, their loose
    sodden slippers sandalled with twine.

They're not lively company at the Dead Letter Office with their try-thats,
    try-thises and not-known-heres.
The barber's brass basin in the last stage of verdigris as I moodle and
    dawdle on this long dismal day.

I'm off to the brick-fields to sift cinders from ashes with a half-bag of
    canvas cobbled with clouts,
drenched and bedraggled, raggled and weary, puckered and woebegone,
    down on my luck.

I can't keep a berth long nor a foot free of bruises, so I'll pawn myself bare
    'til death comes along,
first in the field with my prize of three cat-skins, the thistle and groundsel,
    the rank grassy knots.

My shrivelled leg dangles by the weight of a hob-boot, a dust-yard
    scavenger with a rusty iron sieve,
heaps of brick-breezes and brick-bats and spoil-laths, sheaves of damp
    paper and lost title deeds.

The gypsy cart tilted, the bender tents bended, my bad eye covered by a
foul oyster shell,
my chest heaving ashes that leaves me upended in a commoner graveyard
on a patch of waste-ground.

A cemetery bounded by workhouse and mortar, a bummocky track with
trains screeching past,
the broom and the wild fern, furze and laburnums, nasturtiums and
dahlias, holly-hocks and mad curs.

Wear your best skirt in mourning, trimmed crape and a bonnet, a shawl
or a mantle, dreary grey gloves,
with my bone-bag slung over your shoulder in wonder, the salve and white
powder, chaldrons of coal.

The coarse food and cag-mag fed on by maggots are a sordid reminder of
worms, snails, and slugs
while the bones from the boiler will rattle you over convulsing and
twitching, crushed for manure.

The Song of the Herdsman

Rebuke the beast among the reeds, the fattened lambs and goats,
the curds and milk from herd and flock, stout bulls that besiege
    me.

With horns and hoofs and coarse black hair, fire, jacinth,
    brimstone,
I bow my head next a bulrush marsh nourished by the crag that's
    flinty.

Enter the crypts deep dug in earth, a measure of wheat for a
    penny,
line the walls with the feet of the dead, the fires of hell relieve me.

The Song of the Daysbird

Moulded into being,
I melt beneath your thumb.

A tuft of golden beeswax
I rise to touch the sun.

The Song of the Neander Valley Man

Laid on a Woody Horsetail bed,
turned on my side, both knees flexed,
one hand tucked behind my head,
the other reaching for my axe.
My posture relaxed, my expression vacant
and somewhere off in the distance.

Blanketed with thistle and hyacinth,
my winter-pale skin red-ochre stained,
jasper, shells, bones, foetal flakes of flint,
future remedies to relieve ancient pains.
And next my remains, blue-hued mammoth tusks,
oddly-shaped stones, curios like us.

The Song of the Resurrectionists

We hoist our sacks upon our shoulders and waken the creatures from their
    last sleep,
a little more brandy and if we ever live to die, we'll bury our bodies while

blessing ourselves and muttering paternosters, dropping our bags on the
    other side.
The white tombstone, the ivy-grown church, the hee-haw of an ass, the
    silent hush hush

where the cinder-gatherers gather dust beneath us in the tan-yard of the
    night
for a measly dram, a penny-worth of butter, a mutchkin of whiskey, a
    copper spoon,

or a brass snuff box. Sheep to the shearers, dumb lambs to the slaughter,
    flocks much like us
wrought as bakers, cobblers and weavers, Burkers in the kirkyard shutting
    out the moon,

the watchers paid off and looking on. Us sack-'em-up gentlemen disguised
    in smock-frocks
and fustian jackets, with our crowbars, spades and grappling hooks
    amidst the vaults,

chambers and sepulchres. The markers removed as we exhume a recent
    shallow grave,
the claimed earth loose, the nails unscrewed for the sake of wicked lucre
    and filthy gain.

A rope beneath the oxters and out they bodily pop, the coffin unmoved,
    intact,
the narrow shaft filled up again, the replaced sod of turf. Carrying our
    packs pick-a-back

to the chirurgeon with his eyes and ears in his breeches' pocket, severed
   limb from limb,
carved bone from bone. Us on our way home, like roisterers returning
   from a carouse,

bawdlily singing, *'Burke's the butcher, Hare's the thief, and Knox the boy
   who buys the beef,'*
drudges, scullions, licenced subtlers dealing in teeth, gold rings on our
   fingers, and seals

dangling at our fobs. But better our spoil be dropped and a clean pair of
   heels be shown
than caught in a plaguy ambuscade to suffer a slow death from scaffold to
   gibbet

or like Half-Hangit-Maggie surviving the gallows, galvanised back to life,
   revived
with a score of smart electric shocks, corpses doomed to walk the night
   'til we die of dropsy

or get marked with the pox, buried at our own expense to be dug up again
   by men like us.
Stripped of our shrouds, stuffed in sacks with tuppence-ha'pennies held
   tight in our beastly grasp,

cadaveric spasms down our backs, packed in crates, seasoned, pickled in
   casks of Bitter Salts,
carried on carters down to the docks. Lock us up instead in patent coffins
   made of lead,

and store us in a morthouse until putrid and decomposed, our bones
   vitrified,
our sublimated lives cheating the infested devil out of his infernal due.

The Song of the Borachan

I

He's stiff but he's steady with a plate of clay pipes, the lord-of-mercys, and
    an outlawed
twist of tobacco stacked high on his chest. Him laid out on his hag-bed
    under the table

snuffing gossip out of the depths. While I bandy-legged and bowed sing
    'The Black Stripper'
and 'Nell Flaherty's Drake' playing forfeits, rehearsing the waits. Wake up
    from the wake.

Sobs they sighed on a dry and thirsty morning. Well they can't say,
    'without warning'.
Despite where we're heading, we know where it's leading. Saving our
    pennies for whiskey and poteen.

Redden your pipe and pray for the souls of the dead, we'll play for the
    souls of the dead,
then kiss the corpse and nail the coffin shut. We don't sheep-steal, but we
    grow good grass.

In from the fields of fancy mud and all the uproar from upturned roofs of
    sod and reeds
and turf be-god. Through the burning bush, the white-thorned scrub
    through rugged woods

where the hooded women stoop for herbs and other such-no-goods,
    barefoot in the flooded
swollen streams, the muddied brooks, torch lit, and we knew the dark the
    best we could.

Over the mountains, across the pass, down through the hungry fields, out
    of the famished bogs

into the living ditch, agog at the dish by the door with tobacco, salt and
the lord preserve us.

II

The blackguards with their dirty feet, the cow, the bull and the sleepless
sheep.
A sip of the *Uisce Beatha*, and I'll be with-ya, Turning the Spit and Selling
the Pig,

Drawing the Ship Out of the Mud and the wailing women devout of their
minds
venting the furious in spurious tirades with the why-did-you-dies and the
half-civilised,

the howling thief leaving me to reap and plough my furrow with my
children to weep,
the three crucified leaps of the Virgin-Marys and the why-did-you-beat-
mes and otherwise cheat me.

Another wee sip and a nip of the hard stuff and Hurry the Brogue when
the old ones falter,
on to their beds while we're off to the altar with five lighted candles and
the host in a halter.

Sitting down in a circle, the ghost in the middle, our legs pulled up and
the shoe under-hidden,
him torn asunder trying to find where it isn't, his hand up the skirts of the
women god-willing.

It isn't no wonder when another more younger takes the brogue in his left
hand with actions unbidden

and takes to the hitting the one who's bent-over a crack on his backside
  below his pullover.

III

Then we're Making the Ship from the bodies of men, down on our heels
  laying the keel,
the stern and the stem, and a young innocent lass raising the mast with
  gestures obscene

while a blindfolded shite is Holding the Light to be flogged as a Christ in
  profane travesty.
The Cow and the Bull and the shamed nudity for all plain to see, with the
  corpse looking in,

playing along Riding the Ass with a grasp of the noose and it thrown
  loose over the rafter
and soon thereafter the Donkeys and Baskets, and in comes the weaver
  and all true believers,

Robert Sagart the priest with his robes made of straw and his stole a
  sugain, his great Paidrin
just spuds on a string with a frog for a cross. But all is not lost, it's out
  that he's tossed,

no match for me the bórachán king. He'll drink his own drink this fine
  evening.
While the girls in the corners with their faces scowling, like Sheela na Gigs
  with skeletal ribs,

are already undressing for the boys who've been messing and giving them
  digs,
their clothes away peeled, the forbidden revealed, their huge genitalia in
  alarming extension.

[20]

And no one's relenting to the head on the bed with his eyes opening as he
    makes his ascension
with the beggars full blessing, 'May you all have raggedy children aplenty.'

The Song of the Wet Nurse

Sleep my babies, sweetly sleep, the kind of sleep from which you wake,
the high tide caught between your legs, your head upon an oaken stake.

Bitter cold arise search out the dead, thou art like him leg and chin,
hold thy way though black his face, my dark dark dove with snow-white
    wings.

The slur and gibber of muted birds, loud-mouthed, sulky, cantankerous,
your eyes to open solely for death, the nightingale to mourn your loss.

The cradle-snatcher stalks your field, threatens sore to take your life,
your mother-tongue you shall not hear, when Daddy's drunk he'll share
    his knife.

Your white head turns to face the dawn, your baby rattle won't ward off
    ghosts,
oh, child abandoned eaten by wolves, the girl from the mountain fetters
    your horse.

Black's the life we lead with you, your limbs struck by the serpent's tail,
a fence of stone becomes your tomb, tossed by the winds, lost to the
    waves.

The hawk will steal you from your nest, child alone on a patch of grass.
While you suck blood from both my breasts, your mother's gone out and
    will never come back.

VISIONS

Vision of the Other World
Inspired by the works of Francisco de Quevedo

Astrologers, alchemists, crack-brained fools.
Petty-foggers cutting thongs out of other men's leather,

boring their noses with hot irons, biting their nails to the quick.
Gawdy coxcombs and hob-nailed boots, scythes and sheep-hooks.

Contented cuckolds with pincers, crane-bills, scissors, saws.
Bare-necked women and all sorts of gee-gaws.

Jilts, cheats, picklocks, trepanners, tooth-drawers
picking a quarrel with their gums. Rooks and jackdaws,

sons of whores, crook-fingered and baker-legged, cramp-jawed
knaves and fools with their tongues steeped in oil.

Catch-poled blockheads.
The bones I speak of are dead.

Vision of a Sudden Death

Almanacs, globes, spheres, astrolabes. Strokes of lightning, violent rains,
tempest, plague and pestilence. Wars, discords, conspiracies smeared

with the filth of the fountain. Some swimming, others wading or
    drowning.
Relentless furies and sly seducers bedewed with floods of tears. The
    incognito

seized and fettered in all of its infernal forms, the grand ascent of
    penitential
retrospects, frauds and larcenies, the infidelities weighted down. Squared-
    off

predictions for a groat apiece, a purchased glimpse into futurity. The
    horror
of a sudden death. Embroideries, brocades, damasks, rags. Landaus,
    coaches,

packs of hounds. Runners on foot following the chase, the long-sought
    prize
eluding vigilance. The poorer sort. Mad pursuers with plodding steps,

hags, halberdiers at a captain's place. Mattock and spade, blackbird and
    thrush,
the devil sneezing on a pinch of snuff. Planets falling from their off-kilter
    orbits,

afflicted moons of gluttony, debauchery and wantonness. Pedestals,
    columns,
cornices, friezes, architraves, chapters in half-relief shook from the
    foundations

of their belief, sent to early graves. Bankrupts 'in subterranean abodes,'
and hautboy notaries. Sober-tongued scrimshanders of rhinoceros horn

and trephined skulls, cups for wine, aqua ardens, aqua fortis, vinum
    adustum.
Poleaxed horses in a knacker's yard. An armametarium of glass shards,
    flint,

shark's teeth, and bone. Pomatums of rosin, pitch and terebinth,
    strychnia,
stramonium, clove oil, bitter almond. Cabbagers of rotten luck made mad

on bhang and arrack. Glasses pricked with acid, the stupefying bitter
    stuff. Molasses,
copperas, cocculus indicus, mendacious flatterers hard as the rocks of
    Parnassus.

Vision of Quicksilver

The women of Smyrna swallowing drams of Mediterranean mercury
to plumpen up their charms, legendary beauties desired for Turkish
   harems.

The flying carpet Oriental romance of Spice Island false pregnancies.
Children made orphans by bloody massacre returning in vain to the
   fruits

and the flowers of the Sultan's invitation. Their wounds still bleeding,
the wild beast's paw upon them, their own blood moistening the orchids

growing over their fathers' graves. The women outside the walls, shaded
by the groves of a funereal tree, arranging their shawls to hide their
   faces

beneath a mourning cypress. The perfumed East ingesting quicksilver
in pursuit of comeliness. A laxative trail of bejeweled globules scattered

on the ballroom floor gathered by black eunuchs in the sweepings
of the withdrawing room. The orange trees in full and vivacious bloom.

II

A coffee house fronting the harbour where cross-legged dragomen sit
smoking the chibouk, military coats, cocked-hats and canes, doubloons

and Spanish dollars. An African marked with the smallpox, the sirocco
blowing in his teeth. Tassels, festoons of artificial flowers, gold leaf.

Vests of velvet bound around the waist, confined with clasps of silver,
embroidered zones. A lame footed social castrate, a literal basket case,

two pistols and a yataghan in his belt. Transvestite boy dancers with
    rouged
complexions. Pale dowagers roaring quarantino, simulating contractions,

sered toads in their armpits and groins drying out their sores. Barbers
    shaving
off their pilgrims' body-hair, bowdlerised into damsels, cross-dressing
    wives

travelling in Arab caravans through dangerous desert dunes. Women
    garbed
in sailor-suits kissing older married men. Their lost and wandering
    wombs.

III

Red earth, burnished steel, white gold. Antimonious cupellation tinged
into pure silver fermentation. The hidden city, the locus of desire,

water washing out the earth, the excess strained in a twisted buckskin
    bag.
The pan and cradle abandoned by the honest miners, leaping barefoot

over heaps of brayed metal, beds of fire. Jumping their claims for cheap
labour and enterprise, a mild muriate, pay dirt thrown in with worn
    shovels.

Decrepit mules made frisky by gypsy horse-traders, rearing their heads
to shake the noise from their skulls. Mirror-silverers with trembling limbs

stirring the depravity of their actions. Amalgams prepared with silver
    powder
pressed into drilled decaying holes. The solid flight of liquid gravity.

Incoherent, vaporous, evanescent. Photographic plates rapturous with
    breath.
An incandescent act of light reflecting back its own glaring absence.

Vision of Death's Virtues

Beat a drum covered in wolf skin:
a sheep is made afraid.

Beat a drum covered in bear skin:
the horses run away.

Lay the hyena beside the panther:
the hide loses its hair.

Finger the harp strings made from catgut:
bring no comfort to the ear.

Slay the birds and beasts together:
their blood will not be shared.

Vision of The Fear of Death

Set the hounds at the oxen,
let the prey upon them.

Flush the pheasants from the tules,
loose the hawks and falcons.

Cast the peacocks from the tower,
quaking as they plummet.

Baste the carcass on the slab,
made tender in the fear of death.

Vision of Light and Shadow

'Light, more light'
Goethe's dying words

Light, more light. The shadow of the sun turns back on the dial. A rod
    into a serpent,
iron floating on water. The hysteria of prophecies, clairvoyance, magnetic
    sleep.

Letters read while confined to the bed hidden beneath the sheets. Spirit-
    drawings,
tongues and abstruse theories, chest cramps, haemorrhaging, loss of teeth.
    A ring

of metal lying heavy on the nerves, the lamp dug deep to illuminate the
    world.
Light, more light. Muslin secreted within underclothes, instruments
    rattling

behind cabinet walls. Voices bellowing through paste-board speaking-
    trumpets,
the dim-lit spirit-forms. Masks, wires, telescopic rods, wax hands, veils,
    and shawls.

The stock in trade of every third-rate conjurer. Apports and deports. Slate
    writing,
table rapping. The destined apparatus of deceit. The sitter and the medium
    holding

hands, pressing feet. A chair rising towards the ceiling. A body slowly
    levitating.
Light, more light. The mind abruptly gravitating, a voice corruptly speaks.

Vision of the Healer

Saintly tombs, holy relics, patent nostrums, electric belts. A talisman,
a penance, a laying on of a layman's hands. An Adam's apple bulging
    from

a sweet orange seed, pressing through the throng of citrons and bitter
    lemons
to touch the healer's heathen robe. Unhoped for, sudden and prodigious
    cures.

The imperative will of the operator filled with facts of this nature.
An auxiliary crucifix, fire-philosophers, disembodied men summoned

under the Vagrant Act. Profane utterances surcharged with passion,
prodigies and illusions, child prophets, seers, poets, fakirs buried alive.

A dead daughter floating in a bright liquor, resolved into a vapour.
    Phantasms
of thinking throblets mouldering like antiquated trash. Thrums of lapis
    asbestos

placed in a Venetian glass, set in sand, the wick anointed and besmeared.
Brothers, sisters, husbands, wives, hired men lodged together underneath

the threadbare sheets, their heads turned northwards during a fitful sleep
repulsing the nervous electrical charge. Direct magnetic lines,
    melancholia,

paralysis, softening of the brain, infantile complaints, diseases of the
    heart.
Partial sweats, mild anxiety, sudoriferous, diaphoretic, blue-pill diuretics.

Steel and bark. Recessed galleries, balconies, nooks and corners of the
    mind

tricked out with vines. The etiology of diseases, miasmatic causes,
   contagions.

Double-vision, cachectic states, fetid breath, cramps, vertigo, human
   waste.
Peasants in the field engaged in labour beyond the reach of the
   microscope,

the most enlightened chemist. Angelica, butter-bur, goats' rue,
   masterwort,
poeny, sickly ships anchored off the coast, absorbent vessels, sepulchral

perpetual lamps. Meteoric appearances, atmospheric causes, regimes of
   weather.
Incessant snow, torrential rain, violent hurricanes prevailing over foreign
   seas.

Delirium, intoxication, somnambulism, reverie. Winds, frost, fog. Hogs
   buried
under thirty feet of chalk, lizards embedded in fossilised rocks, toads
   nibbling wood

in the rotten hearts of trees. Bagnio-keepers bleeding, dressing ladies' hair
   on bathing.
Illiterate shavers, apothecaries living on the scent of flowers and Latin
   verses.

Leechcrafters following armies sucking venom, wounds swelling, maggots
   pullulating.
Priests in their sacerdotal cloths in lepers' dwellings. Purified curses, self-
   flagellation.

Vision of the Journey to Hell

With a bed ready for me in hell, I trample the grass of my grave,
lay upon it and send out to pasture three hornless cows,

force my attentions upon a woman come lately from the other side.
She sucks off my ear, hands to me my bow.

Plant yews to the north of us and divide us with their branches.
In time they intertwine, unite us in our grieving, discard our broken vows.

Vision of the Future

After The Various and Ingenious Machines of Agostino Ramelli

The text white on blue, an aqueous coating of ferro-gallate, clamped
    under glass.
Spirit-scripts playing tricks on the eyes, Arabic numerals, glossolalias.

Minute images of healing. Birthing-centres inoculating our senses.
Dispensatories and shops of medicine. Makers of glass, grinders of
    lenses.

Ciphers, codes, baths with nudes. Voynich tubes telescoping our gaze
    into the future.
The machine outside the garden gate lifting its own weight. Techne,
    homo faber.

Water rising under its own power. Legless human bodies twirled on
    stems.
The hand that grasps, directs and pulls reshaping lives. Grotesque
    gargoyles, goblins, worms.

Pulleys hoisting and gears shifting. Winches, pistons, flywheels, hand-
    cranks, treadmills, bellows.
Pontoons, cofferdams, grain-mills, and cranes. The counterpoise of a
    trebuchet that throws

rocks, grows wings. Screw-jacks spreading the bars of portcullises.
    Future forced openings
to distant worlds. Perpetual clocks. Mechanical birds that move their
    heads and sing.

Vision of Rust

Ferrous filings heated in a closed damp crucible exposed to
   animal effluvia.
An airtight mass caulking the rims, pipe sockets packed with
   rings of spun yarn.

Borings, turnings, salt ammoniac, vertical brackets bolted to the
   baseplate, fixed
to the bearing for overhead girders. Flanges concealed with
   ornamental foliage,

metal leaves cast from the true fit of iron bedded on iron. Burrs,
   snugs, stubs.
Oxydised barrels of cider, vinegarised bungholes open to the air.
   Baths of water

acidulated with sulphuric acid in leaden or wooden vessels, tubs
   settling on mud
at ebb tide, bilge and keel, midship-sulphuretted hydrogen and
   alkaline sulphides.

The washspace plumbago of chaffed chains, pintles and eyes, an
   anchor galvanised,
rivet heads highly wrought and refined, scoured with sand,
   deposited in lime.

Plunged into fused zinc, bent and warped out of shape. Nodules
   and carbuncles.
Plumpen oatseeds sown broadcast on sandy loam, mildew,
   blight, wireworm.

Earthen substances sponged and brushed, smoothed through
   bran and sawdust.
Bricks, potters clay, the surface glaze of Babylonian iron-stained
   fictile wares.

Vision of the House of Dust

Ashes, soot, filth, blood, offal, manure. Sewers, cesspools, abattoirs,
    privies.
Cities buried in their own debris. Impassable, decayed. Accessible only
to archaeologists, geologists, butchers, poulterers, fishmongers, bone-
    grubbers.
Restorers of human dust. Conchites, pectinites, ostracites. Shells of former
    selves.

Veins of marble, lapis lazuli, antimony, cinnabar. Fossilised remains.
Plastic virtue latent in the earth. Sens naturel. A swallow's nest, a spider's
    web,

active immortality. Petrified birds hatching petrified young. Vis formatrix,
Archaeopteryx, the missing link. The ventricle, thorax, diluvial shattering

of an alluvial world. Mountains rising from the sea. The omphalos
    hypothesis
of septic grime. Arsenic impregnated clothing trailing in dirt. Layers of
    skirts,

petticoats. Night soil men carting buckets of human waste. Holdmen
    descending
into the pit to loosen shit and shovel it for ropemen to haul up, tubmen

to unload for fertilised fields of muck. The stain of grain-dust, the
    obscuration
of stars. An interstellar extinction of light, absorbed and scattered in sun-
    cracks.

Ripples, rill-marks, beds of sand. Shingle hardened into stone along the
    seashore.
Tilobites, crinoids, worms. Lupus marinus. The encyclopedia of Pliny.

Dog-Heads, sciapodiae, Mouthless Astomi. Bottlenecks, tollbooths,
   blocked streets.
Cattle herded into crowded markets. Corpses cast in ditches with token
   service.

Vision of a Violent Death

The sod cut beneath the feet, stretched out, damnably shaken,
dragged behind a chariot with ankles bound in spancels.

The hair shorn from poll to neck, boast made and spoils taken.
A blow cleaved into the crown, driven to the navel.

Vision of the Danse Macabre

I

A tango of tripudists and caperers dancing the shameless steps of nuns
and friars
in the bars and brothels of the megalopolis for years on end, a morbid
milonga

of itinerant organ-grinders, dockyard violins, and barrel-house paper-
combs
playing out the jerky contortions of the wake in conventillos, urbane
ballrooms

of tenement courtyards, until buried waist-deep in the cold earth. Forget
the wantonness,
the brawls and frays of brewsters and tapsters, flirtatious alewives
strumpeting

overpriced beers, their measures undersized, their kisses excessively free.
Take my hand, and I will lead you away from the cucking-stool to the
churchyard

of the innocents where the capon is larded and skewered upon the spit, the
cook
having split before it could be roasted. Let's dance cheek to bony cheek,
raise a toast

to the alabaster statue, the compadrito, the guapo, the blind guide
summoning
the female mourner, the man falling from the tower, the watch-guard
warming

himself by the fire. We'll dance together like a pair of lovers playing hot
cockles

and mussels, your head laid low in my lap while I strike you a strenuous
  blow

to free the butterfly from your envious mouth. Let the shepherd sitting on
  the stone
save you from the sensuous grave, his foot upon the world, playing a
  dubious tune

on his double flute, the black man with his trumpet on the vaulted roof.
  Flesh-peddlers
in slouch hats, loosely tied kerchiefs, knives beneath their belts, and high-
  heeled boots.

II

Oh my lady, my betrothed, my galley slave, my Cardinal and Pope, the
  fresco has decayed,
the dog snatched up, his lead cut, his master set loose into the forest where
  three youths

hunt him down. Oh beggar, peasant, soldier, Jew, oh widow, cantor,
  jurist, pauper,
oh merchant, minstrel, ploughman, doctor, I'll tease the bull with your
  merry daughter,

drink wine from the bursting caskets, plunder the tinker's baskets, a plate
  of viands, faggots,
a tray of drinking glasses. Seize the city maiden, take the housemaid's
  broom, lay hold

of the forlorn midwife, the infant newly born. We'll shear the sheep and
  prune the tree.
Wood cuts, folios of leaves. Reap the velum, thread the needle, drink from
  a leathern bottle,

throttle the fraudulent innkeeper, his adulterated cask of liquor, pull the
    grave digger
into the grave he has been digging and strike the bride with a scythe and
    sickle. I'll dance

the phrase, lean your way, leave measures in the air, evading the
    stumbling counterbeat.
Slumming in my jackboots, I'll strike my drum in double time with your
    slight and limber bones.

Vision of Time

A clepsydric float uniformly raised suspended by a chain coiled around an
    axis,
counterpoised by a weight. A hand revolving on a dial-plate. Calibrated
    sticks

of incense burning at a constant rate. The canonical hours of monastic life
    struck
eight times daily on a tower bell heard far beyond the confines of the
    cloister.

The cockcrow late for the call to matins. A horologist drawing
    astronomical rations
for one week's work. A mechanical cosmos of jousting knights, striking
    jacks,

wheels of fortune. Models of the moon and sun. Automata. A planisphere
revealing the constellations. The procession of monks, smiths, carpenters,
    masons,

plasterers, bell-founders, craftsmen in Ptolemaic planetary motion. The
    commotion
of the observers' coordinates, the unequal hour-lines, the period of the
    pendulum

dependent on its expansion and contraction, the friction of its swing
    through air.
Resonator, pacemaker, accumulator. An escapement converting the
    continuous

into discrete harmonious steps. Into the two abysses of infinity and
    nothingness.
The theatrical counterfeit of perfunctory man, the terminal simulacrum of
    his being.

Vision of the Afterlife

A cabin clad in boughs and turf clumped in women's nakedness
with nectar warmed like raw cow cud and lumps of bainne clábair,
the horses dying of themselves and not for want but pleasure.

Among these gallants expect no bed, the partridge has been clobbered
open the vein and drink the blood, the food and lodging's coshered.

Vision of the Blind Beggar

Rogues and vagabonds, gatherers of alms, a hawker's basket with oil-
    cases,
cutlery, trinkets, braces. Ballad singers half-naked, broken-down
    tradesmen,

shipwrecked sailors, all with false papers. A silver spoon they will not
    stumble over.
Potboys and waiters, takers to the rambling life. Sleights of hand, buckle
    and thong,

cards, dice. Ten to a room, two to a bed, shambling refuges for the
    homeless,
lodged in the unions. Foot scamps on the foot-pad rig, ken-crackers,
    daisy-kickers,

queer bit makers. Fidlum bens with fishhooks for fingers, chaunter culls,
    kiddy-
nippers, steel bar flingers snipping off pocket-bottoms with a pair of
    scissors.

Blue pigeon flyers cutting lead from a prayer book to a bible. Jibbers the
    kibbers
fixing lanthorns on a horse's neck. Morning, evening and upright sneaks.
    Jigger dubbers,

lumper-thieves. Low gaggers, sham leggers, rum draggers, levanters.
    Lully-priggers
lifting linen. Hook and snivey with nix the buffer. Sharpters, snitchers,
    prad borrowers,

rum snoosers, queer rosters. Beggars and vagrant imposters. Peterers
    cutting off
portmanteaus, snavellers coaxing children up by-alleys to grabble their
    satchels.

Crocussing doctors and doctresses. Young fry of boys practising at the
    buz napper.
Cadgers, staggering belief, casting glasses and gin measures in knit jackets
    and trowsers.

Bowsers vomiting waspish and dyspeptic spleen, dastardly pitiful schemes,
sent to their last account with all the imperfections on their hazardous
    heads.

Cattle drovers and pot hawkers slaking their thirst with water. Vendors of
    pens, paper,
spectacles, laces, razors. Distributors of religious tracts. Manslaughtering
    servants

of medical quacks. Card sellers at the races. Lurkers as butchers, tallow
    chandlers,
curriers, preachers screeching on village streets. Gurriers praying for their
    bread,

cheese, beer, and bed. The fallen sick, died and buried, coming back to
    life.
Their own sons and daughters, mothers, sisters, idiot brothers, aged
    fathers.
Polishers, mangleturner's, blowers in blacksmith's forges. Chaff choppers
    for horses.
Butter churners forced to the streets for living and trade, knocking their
    sticks

as though awake. Women labourers making pies and puddings, sent to the
    oven
handy and quick, sweeping the floors without leaving a speck, whitening
    the hearth,

black-leading the grate, dressing the chimney piece handsome.
   Chancers chancing.
The blind leading the merry blind. Men and women marrying their
   own sightless kind.

Vision of the Camera Obscura

The crystalline lenses of minnows and fallfish, thin delicate films of
   albumen.
A meniscal loupe exposing the Garden of Eden through a minute
   aperture,

a dark chamber known to pharaohs and Arabian nights. The scattered
   rays
of sunlight. An argand burner in a magic lantern, glass globules melted

in a spirit lamp. Mirrors, anamorphoses, optical boxes, dioptric
   paradoxes.
A phantasmagoric stroboscopic effect. The visual persistence of inventors,

faddists, reckless dabblers. A quattrocento fixing of the image of life.
Light-sensitive photographic plates, exact historical dates, the synthesis

of motion. Living figures on the screen. The strolling sauntering gaze
of the converging surface, the concave mirror of transparent focus.

Shadow views of the sciopticon, kinetoscopes, phenakistiscopes,
zoetropes, cogged wheels, and the nickel slots of Edison illuminating

the Promethean dream of practical men. A wide angle, the telephoto end.
The blinding of a distanced monocular eye. Camera, crew, lights and
   scene,

frame-lines, cuts and joins. The desiderata of portable apparatus, shells,
cameos, coins. A human hand and face. Panoramic dioramic space.

Dissolving views of the peepshow. Oil, coal-gas, oxy-hydrogen limelight,
combustible frames bursting into incandescent flames. Perspectiva
   artificialis.

Vision of the House of Ill-Repute

The madhouse, gibbet and gaol. The lingering doubt of hell-fire preaching.
Hades craters, fuliginous flames, demoniacal ravens. Satan bottling

an unquenchable elixir. Anatomists, chemists, microcscopists,
    apothecaries,
retailers of spirituous, vinous and malt liquors. Disorderly, ill-governed
    resorts

of the idle and dissolute. The well-possessed, common nuisances,
    vagrants.
Houses of ill-repute and fame. Illegal gamers without written consent.

Drovers driving horses, cattle, mules, and hogs through herds of stock.
Grotesque young ladies assailed in public places, deliriously fermenting

importunities of loathsome young debauchees, holding up an hourglass
to fill a large vat with vitriol. Mothers inside a trap feeding gin to babies.

Two-headed barmaids with skeletal feet. The groggery, muddle and stupor
of stramonium, cocculus indicus, caustic potash, sulphuric acid, toper.

Dogs dying with cruel convulsions, fish stupifying in strychnined streams.
The virulence of fusel oil, Jersey lightning. Poisoners and poison mongers.

Antinomian Christians, skirmishers, sharp-shooters, and arch-traitors.
Coal-pickers, compositors, corset makers. Screaming seducers, tempters,

and piteous knaves. Dram-sellers hiding their light under a bushel.
Tent revivalists speaking in tongues, drunken glossolalia for our sober
    sins.

Vision of the Dead Land

Here in the dead land, the claw land, the taxis of Saigon, the rickshaws
   and traffic,
the shrunken heads, severed hands and penises, corpses pierced with
   shrapnel.

Bones from restaurants and butcher houses, shreds of meat teeming with
   maggots,
eggs crunched within the hands, the whites slithering between the fingers,

a thousand yellow suns bursting in the sky, sunshine units exploding in
   the air.
All sons of bitches now. The shatterer of worlds, the unalterable yes,

the small piece of earth we do not want to lose. The fraudulent game of
   dice
stripping away our possessions. Fire-bombings and island-hopping
   invasions,

submarine attacks, slippery and entangled, body-snatching baby-bones
to serve our country well. Calmly strapped in chairs in light-tight trailers,

upshot knothole, meticulously blinded by the absolute end of time.
The exponential proliferation of the future, its garage sale of ailing
   devices,

the conceptual force of the sublime, blasting, pouncing, boring its way
   through.
A vision seen to last forever, shielded only by welding glasses, goggles,
   barriers,

miles of buffer zones in the cold desert morning, registering in the
   misaligned
instruments of the body. Warheads, shells, torpedoes, and depth charges.

Kodaks and Brownies. Unofficial snapshots of girl-scouts in polished
  saddle Oxfords,
a man pounding on a red tom-tom, a boy bouncing on his father's
  shoulders,

a head rising from the swamp, coconut trees viewed through the veil of
  coloured smoke
wafting through the frame, the dailies and rough cuts, sneak previews
  filled with sailors

looking for a good time. The white blaze stretching to the still-dark skies,
  the jade green glass
left cratered behind. The blind girl seeing the future, witnessing the past
  from 240 miles.

Gasoline, benzene, polystyrene plastic, skeltering canisters dropping from
  horrible skies.
Flaming globs of jellied-fuel, shameful gobs of melted skin, napalm-
  blackened hands.

Babies deformed with mushroom-clouded heads, the warped jaws welded
  to their chests.
The gangrened fingers and toes, the obscene pain, the intolerable weight
  of air upon the flesh.

MEDITATIONS

Take Me Out to the Lowgrounds

I'm not afraid of lazy men in velvet fronted waistcoats / the elevated
    churchyard crowded
with overgrown graves / the sloops laden with war-stores / nor convict
    boatmen on hulks
that never sail / penal colonies swinging elbow to elbow on hammocks
    amongst the decaying

ribs / contorted in their felon dreams / Tailors, weavers, shoemakers
    scraping the rust from shells
and stacking timber / cleaning guns and shot, spinning and balling oakum
    / cutting up old rope /
What hope is there for me aboard my lowly vessel / hang my shirt instead
    on the rigging

black with vermin, peppered with cholera / Take me out to the
    lowgrounds where cattle
find shelter / where the upset barrow carries no load / and bury me in the
    marshes
in a place unknown / where the convict's flower blooms pale blue before
    the cold

This the Day of Slaughter

The wild grape is in bloom and the air filled with its perfume / the
    piercing cries of the manic
oppressed and desolate / I do not claim the poor and crazed who pine in
    stalls and cages /
the waste-rooms we are acquainted with / the road shaded and cool, oak
    trees bathed in moss /

nor the suffering creature shut out and cut off / the blackberries picked
    from the roadside /
plum-laden branches / hominy and crabs, wood ticks and fleas / I have
    seen the bones of rats,
owls caught in the garret, men drowned at sea / the clouds pitch their tent
    about them

while I labour in a field of wheat / all sixty acres to be cradled beneath the
    relentless heat
of a southern sun / This is what I have become, carrying my seed bag so I
    may sleep on grass /
I have sold my horse for a petty sum / black geese and a flock of prairie
    hens / I am the one

who seeks asylum now / When all is done I will slip the leg-holds and the
    collars free,
buy nine yards of tow and linen, a bushel of corn meal / soak my
    lacerations in salted water,
watch the flesh creep / the deal complete / the mortifications of this the
    day of slaughter

3

The Hour is Upon Us

In the silent darkness I rise, turn on the light / break out from the privacy
    of sleep which is still
to come / You rest on / how gone is gone / I watch you lie beneath the
    sheets / I hear you speak
'We are decaying' / and you are scarcely breathing, and I am scared / In
    your uncommon tongue

the fleeting night compares to nothing I have ever known / I pace the room
    / outside the curtained
window the silhouette, Chaplinesque / I think I hear music / Satie,
    Stravinsky, Schönberg, Poulenc /
the poems of Rimbaud, Verlaine / and in the corners, the shadows, Alfred
    Stieglitz / and off your lips,

poète maudit / the cursed themes / From your shoulders the blanket slips,
    and this is it / you vault
the rails and scorn the wake of the lingering ship / the life preservers cast
    overboard, the life-boats
lowered / some say an arm was raised / what's done is done / a body
    turned in a sudden wave /

What is it you are saying / dawn is still so far away / and on the blank and
    single page the terror struck /
I can't hear you / we were born too early, we were born too late / the lilacs
    in the dooryard know
your form / the dark trails fingers down your neck as though to
    compensate / and I regret / Forget

the flesh that drapes and then collects / we know no bliss / breadlines,
    handouts, beggars on stoops,
a hand-pump for water, an outhouse out back, an explosion of shouts and
    fists / I could turn down

the light / hold your wrist and sit beside you on the bed / the dread like a
   kiss cold and underfed /
What is it we feel anymore / our sensibilities blunted by the shock of
   excess / The harbour beacon
darkens, brightens, darkens / the off-shore winds blow the shutters open
   and shut / I fill the room
with exotics / roses, lilies, acanthus, bells in their towers / my love, the
   hour is upon us

4

Beyond the Dead

The high ones die, die / and I am on the wire / with blackouts and
    delirium tremens /
shake yourself out of it / we have to die / we may as well be up there one
    foot unsteadily
in front of the other / maintaining our balance / This is not some kind of
    fit / an idiot

in a Swiss sanatorium / abandoned in a drying-out ward / You heard me,
    we have to die /
the brief pulse of the electrodes on either side of the head / the IV drip
    convulsing
beside the bed / the black worms crawling up the walls / the palpitations
    and sweats /

insects burrowing beneath the skin / the appalling nerves, the panic
    attacks / Relax /
we have to die / a lifetime of deception / standard royalty terms and
    advance / I do not
want to go beyond the dead / what of mental unrest / perhaps that's better
    left unsaid /

but up there on the wire in the dark / a pole to amplify my sway / without
    the lure
of safety nets / the bounced cheques / Entranced by the saccadic
    movements
of my eyes / I lift one foot in front of the next / a wayward step

You Won't Awake
i.m. John Berryman

What I fear most is going insane / that would be the death of me /
    existential anxiety /
The vitamins, drugs, anticonvulsants as repulsive as lubricious chorus
    girls /
or buxom hostesses at the gates of Hell / a dead porcupine, a sea urchin,
    clams /

It's out of our hands / like night-starts at the onset of sleep / Chaucer,
    Tennyson, Gray /
This much I will say / the thought jerked me from my drowsy state / you
    won't awake /
to stand forever in the stag line lost for honeys / at an out-of-time
    speakeasy

with my coat checked in / I really don't know how to dance / Byron,
    Shelley, Keats /
there is no romance / 'and the truth you shall deliver of that be not afraid'
    / but I am
afraid, scared beyond belief / I don't know how to dress for New York
    fashion /

what clothes to wear when on the street / wing-tipped sport Oxfords with
    leather heels /
the Hunt Club at West Forty-Fifth / Martinis and ginger ale, the nakedest
    floor show
you have ever seen / cute hussies with rolling eyes, huge asses and plump
    breasts /

Application, catechism, arithmetic / 'Goodnight Sweetheart' and all the
    rest /
a young boy lost amidst the illicit burning flesh / The night is black as sin /
the doorman beckons me in

The Air Does Not Willingly Serve Us Breath
i.m. Hart Crane

I guess I didn't feel the best / an autumn stroll through the wastelands of
    Cramp's
deserted shipyard / having finally escaped the wreck of the steamship
    SS Orizaba /
undesired, underhauled and slowed by drag / Forget the slag heaps
    sintered in the bath /

the half-naked sledge-swingers so damned dead / the molten plates of
    red-hot metal
bent in and out of shape / I should not have done exactly what I did / If
    God would permit
it, the pit would not have opened / the sword be whet / There are in the
    souls of wicked men

lines laid down in the mold loft, oft repeated / those who would stand
    upon the burning deck
salute the acres of their own contrivances / rusted by the sweat of
    abandoned men
subject to the bondage of their own corruption / I forget now where I
    started out from /

the keel laid on mammoth blocks / the fore and aft, stern-post and
    sacrificial ram /
but here is where I am / the air does not willingly serve us breath / creation
    groans
beneath our burden / Down Palmer Street and Petty's Island where plans
    were hatched /

I turned my back / and in the swift few seconds it takes to launch this heft
    of steel /
the timbers greased with tallow / I sink without a trace / Let's face it,
the water is not shallow and we are out of place

The Hook is Slung

Everyone dies on the way down / from the barstool at The White Horse
    Tavern /
wet brained to the floor / longshoremen standing on the stones /
    confabulating
lives they never lived / the dunnage of their suffering keeping them afloat /

We stand vigil or lapse into a coma / only time will show / an oxygen tent
in a darkened room / a wife gone wild lashing and seductive / the boyish
bodies gone to sea / and always, always the infidelities / Locked up

in cold rage / a dead man's coat / what hope is there that we will be
    assuaged /
A swelling of the brain denying oxygen / inflammation of the lung, septic
    shock /
a stopper knot / a docker's hook hauling in our cargo / that lewd and
    brooding

performance drawing in the crowd / mesmerised by the deathly
    possibilities /
the reckless end of an obscene act needing no encouragement / It's a cruel
and lurid fact / the hook is slung / the sinking cargo still intact

8

This After All is Life

In St Elizabeth's Hospital for the Criminally Insane, the poets feign
    madness /
chain themselves to the walls, lie in their own excrement, wear soft
    slippers
to lose their footfalls / retreat to the confessional high strung on
    morphine /

thieving sex from someone else's wife / This after all is life / Down the
    hall
the purges begin / vile concoctions to make the silence vomit / leech
    blood
from the veins / what of it . . .

                          . . . in a moment the warden will turn out the light /
the shifting and shuffling decease / outside the bedlam beggars will rest
in peace / There is no glory in any of this / the kiss exchanged during
    coitus

lies grease-stained on the lips / the hips that bucked in vain / and what
of all that loss / I can't complain / the isolation room is nothing new to
    me /
this time I'll close the door and look back in at where I used to be /
    except

this time there's nothing to be seen / it's as they say / the lunatic asylum
has had its day / and all that now remains, an inmate detached
from his demented brain / Who now to count the cost

9

We Won't Meet Again
i.m. of the massacre at Oradour-sur-Glane

There is no witness to what comes next / what charnel house we heap
 ourselves within /
between the rows of willows and the burnt out church / the charred
 remains of babies
in their prams / the champagne bottles and the emptied purse / the
 segregated women

in the barn / shot in the legs before being set alight / The terror of screams
 in broad daylight /
This then is death / In a dull two-room cinder block apartment, in better
 shape than anyone
had dreamed, you say, *don't say we won't meet again* / It's cunning how
 you stay close

to your God / and brave how you make that stunning leap / I like to think
 the babies are asleep,
the women simply lame / the truth of course is gloomier, I will soon move
 in with them / *the horror*
I have turned to light relief / It's my belief we'll never see the light of day
 again / There are many

ways of looking at a river / and as many ways to pay your way across /
 Don't get me wrong / I don't
expect to reach the other side / the current's strong / and Charon just can't
 stay upon his feet /
Later the soldiers engaged in carnal pleasure to scream the screams away
 in endless sleep

Working the Height

I have trouble and struggle with altitude / a girder-jack having lost my
    nerve / the urgent and intimate
handful of sky within my clutch / You're either hooked to a lifeline or not
    working the height / but tonight
amongst the brigs, barques, brigantines, East Indiamen, ships of the line,
    sloops of war / I ask for balance

to be restored / The yardmen are going aloft, springing into the shrouds,
    the ratlines beneath their feet /
the course yard and the fighting top / 'lay out and loose' / casting off the
    gaskets / 'Let fall, sheet home,
lay in' / the blanket white descends / the brothels, gambling houses, opium
    dens / mast-headed by routine /

reveille, dress, lash the hammocks / loose, reef and furl / my leg wrapped
    around the headache ball /
swung onto the iron without belts or nets / Do not be fooled, I am scared
    of heights / the bucket of bolts
on my shoulder / frozen above the chasm of empty space / bridging the gap
    with steelwork frames / caught

by my own braggart and blowhard fear / Before I forget, the carelessly
    dropped wrench / the glancing blow
to the head / the red hot rivets chucked from forge to girder end / We don't
    die, we get killed / that's a fact /
red numbers painted on the steel as our last act / death hits close to home /
    We are all fucking apprentices

who don't know our ass from a hole in the ground / punking rebar /
    demeaned and castigated / testing

our loyalty for a time of crisis / the Saturday night toot, the Monday
   morning jumping jeepers / the high iron
transformation atop each mast / main, mizzen, fore / where we find our
   feet, stand erect and sail for home

Curtain Call

It's curtain call and the audience has long since departed / strike whatever
    pose you wish /
the applause you meet is silence / Perhaps they are waiting in the cellarage
    at Hell's mouth to spring out when least expected /
or the grave-trap crowing like roosters and baying like hounds / It's
    tempting to clap yourself /

Better that, it's said, than the inn-yards with their bear-baiting pits /
    fending and proving, scratching
and biting by plain tooth on nail / Tread the ground, and you shall hear its
    hollowness / but I regress /
the stone slab is prised open / the bodies of the tragic lovers pulled from
    the jaws of death / the curtain

drawn back on the bridal bed / the seamless transposition of stagecraft
    instead / Meanwhile a troupe
of acrobats defy the draw of gravity / while in the Heavens the ropes and
    rigging engage the lowly
entrance of an ancient god long since forgotten / What can I say / in the
    tiring-house behind the stage

the costume change is seamless / we the audience in on the secret from the
    first / the pageant wagon
not open to the weather / and worse, the double plot written by game-
    writing hacks / all the while
the jousters and fencers, singers and dancers, keepers of fighting cocks /
    the grotesque antimasque,

the impropriety of its dance / a disorder the interludes of masquerades
    cannot transform / for god
nor king / If you must, stamp your foot and all will rise on cue in flashing
    lights / ascend as the lofty

counterweight descends / the satyr leering from the wings / the witling's
 puerile conceit / It's no defeat /

the mountebank's to blame / fooling the penny stinkards in the yard with
 rosin blowing through a flame /
while someone else is paid to imitate the cock that crowed for Peter's
 shame / the false breastplate
has been pierced and bleeds the blood of calves / the curtain falls and that
 is all we have

Nothing is the Matter

There comes a rope hung heavy on the beam of night / I am at a
     loss to know just who
should hang from it / the draggle tailed wench seducing life with
     lusty fervour / or the skip
kennel boy obeying its every flunked up order / never a barrel the
     better herring /

In our talk the stench of its very odour / the torment and dross
     returned with equal favour /
the buffoons have come home to rest / their anacoluthic rack
     stretched until the bones crack
and break asunder / their terrible words do not come back / have
     no respect for dialects /

A hex on hacks / Nothing is the matter / On the ward for
     alcoholics the doors are locked /
the babies have been tossed out with the water from the bath /
     the rhythm sprung
like a heart with a single beat / syllabically weak and slack / kept
     more intact

in the knocking bones, smooth-polished flat / Enough of that /
     the rope hangs heavy
and that's a fact / Nothing is the matter / the heart has sprung a
     leak / and for our part
it would be best if we never chose to speak / silence is where it's
     at

Something Rare
i.m. Randall Jarrell

A favourite pair of gloves / the road narrow and badly lit / the
    head-on glance at windscreen height /
and suddenly he was hit / dead by all accounts / he smoked
    honey-scented tobacco / read Baudelaire /
but that night there the air was filled with something rare / Was
    he killed / it's true no blood

was spilled / Back home I tacked a carpet down and talked of
    going to Tennessee / it's not unknown /
I got a tent and rigged it on my lawn / at dawn the sun came up
    as might have been expected /
what happened next / I took in someone's washing from the line
    simply to inspect it / it's not so

hotsy-totsy but I do inhale the camphor balls and all / like
    parking in a loading zone before cocktails
at the Ritz / Day by day goes by / we're waiting for the hits / and
    we're talking suicide staking out
the highs our words induce / It's quite absurd / this world when
    we get right down to it is for the birds /

there's no end to the flights our feathered friends pretend / Alone
    on the abandoned road did he
have rights / his lights knocked out / It's a shock to the system in
    the end / there's that to think about /
without a doubt I never thought we had it made / in spades, he
    said marking out his trade / He was not

afraid to tell it as it was / and all because we can't be saved
    despite the highfaluting talk of low brigade /
you know he was simply out for his evening walk / or so they say
    / I think he stepped out from the verge /

merged with traffic of a mortal sort / had his wings clipped so to
   speak / a bird of prey without his beak /

We drove home drunk on anxious thoughts / I couldn't say that
   what we sought we ever found /
beneath the carpet the floor was worn down / with feet that
   never quite had touched the ground /
It's hard to sanction the final hour that we crave / *Les Fleurs de
   Mal* spread-eagled on his grave

What I Am Scared of Most is Nothing

The little bird with the woman's face who charms us with her
    song / what's wrong with that /
we could plug our ears with beeswax, tie ourselves to the mast /
    but that can't last / in any case what kills
us in the end is the silence that follows / I know it's hard to
    swallow but what I'm scared of most

is nothing / Stiff and slow with age there's little left besides / the
    singing draws us near but really
who would rest a while with that / I'd serve her gin / wind up the
    gramophone / hear Benny Goodman
spin / 'Sing Sing Sing (with a Swing)' / Better that than shovelling
    hard in the stockyards / stinking to high

Heavens / or falling into the rendering vats / ground up with
    animal parts to be sold as lard / They tell us
it's not a sin / but even the gramophone must wind down / the
    woman drop tired in your arms / soon fall
asleep / it's all the rage / and this is where the end comes in / the
    music fades / the silence of the deep /

One way or another we are all packing meat / it's hard times on
    the killing floor / the nuns have turned
to whores, lure travellers into poverty / not that it bothers me / I
    would rather keep poor company
than sail into that broiling sea / There is nothing I am afraid of /
    I sing when it's stormy, when it's calm I weep

Where Away?

If you see this life as the best death has to offer / you would trade
    it surely for suffering & laughter /
If you wrestle with the wreck of your life / write letters daily to
    your mistress / 'We had it out again yesterday / Damn! Yr
    life is so easy on the way up . . .' / She writes: 'Is that how it
    looks?' / In spite

of this, said he: 'I see nothing else' / Granted / 'At the end of the
    day, do you have any energy left?
Any life for the living?' / Is it enough / This stuff resembles death
    / you can bet your life on that /
She badgers: 'It is a record of fact what happened to the crew of
    the Essex / 21 men sunk

by a sperm whale in the Pacific / 1819 / eating each other in the
    end / Nantucket men
on Nantucket men' / Grins he: 'My point exactly' / What do /
    'Wharves in storms, Amen' /
Much is left unsaid / 'which brings me (&you) / or so I have
    found' / Frowns she: 'the thing

is so dense now' / plus this / and then:'I know we feast on flesh,
    what's new?' / What else
& back we go again / wretched in the extreme / Nor is that all /
    The Nantucket men excreted
each other out their puckered holes / their swollen arses bent over
    the blackened bow /

the putrid stench of fetid diarrhoea / heave her up and away we'll
    go / Far from the naked
Hawaiian women swimming in the port / the Quaker wives of
    the last resort take up their pens /

says they with laughter: 'Where away?' / 'Two points on the
    weather bow' / 'how far off?' /

'a mile and a half' / 'keep your eye on her!' / 'sing out when we
    head right' / then
with suffering: 'Stand by and lower for one a little more than
    half a mile to windward' /
'make good your lay' / 'the men are coming home / gnawing on
    their brothers' bones'

Striving to Stay Alive

If I really am what I say, it is more than weighing my words / and
    I am back to rivers now / where
meanings flow past the point where I stand / the words are
    weighing me / sinkers revealing infidelities,
breakdowns, addictions / It is true that my confessions are bereft
    of mass atrocities / but I dare say . . . /

What exactly is it that I am saying / what exactly is it that I am
    trying to make sense of / late-night
skinny-dipping in the creek / ditching our bathing suits amongst
    the Martini set / I am not making light
of this / but don't you feel it, that chaos in your life / the
    unlivable striving to stay alive / the water

trickling through the stones at the soles of your feet / shifting the
    ground beneath you / It's not
the body of the words that reek decay / but the mind
    decomposing / Suppose, and I am talking
into the wind, but suppose this claim is true / in other words I
    am incoherent / the blood clotting

the veins just so / bruised and raging / On other days I wake up
    terrified / the page conceals the pen /
We have reason to be afraid / I have endured the ferocity of the
    imagination / its confusion in the end . . . /
Pretend I never said these things / it's true the real delusion is
    thinking we can say what we intend

Profuse With Darkness

The wires have burnt out / intense, unworldly / the waterlogged
  third rail cable / 750 volts
that jumped and sent a jolt from track to signal-switching tower /
  our brains derailed
in the surge / igniting into catastrophe / Is this the way it has to
  be / the tortured minds

syntactically profane / a childhood form of asthma the oxygen
  tent cannot contain /
In a winter of extreme cold, ill, isolated, in despair / us with our
  freshly cut hair / horn-rimmed
glasses, sleeveless sweaters / impeccably dressed / we confessed to
  nothing except our own

weaknesses / If it turned out the train was late but not delayed,
  would that change anything /
The current flowing from the fuse / I am not much use, I am
  afraid / in deciphering the things
I have been saying / except to say I never meant it that way / The
  tunnel long, profuse with darkness /

the discharged electrical sparks incandescent in a body cold and
  perfectly black / This then is
the way back / the crippling uncertainty we cannot track / the
  note of triumph is never struck /
and us / respectable / refuse the blame / the dead cannot read the
  elegies written in their name

Indulge in Dying

Let us stand out in the thunderstorms to be struck by lightning /
    not once but . . . /
who is ready to admit defeat / the naked vulnerability askance /
    ensconced in doubtful self-belief /
a fitting sentimentality to shore up survival / At our core we
    indulge in dying /

death's other great rival / I am not blind to the trivial or the
    insignificant / the wooded by-pass
of memory / but up ahead of me the light is doused / the cows
    come home ignoring grunts
and unfamiliar noises / gnawing on the wet grass through which
    the current spreads /

in through their mouths and out their legs / eating away at their
    own death / chewing on its cud /
I should intervene / Listen to me / what if the thunder never
    comes / if the darkness is stunned
into silence / or better yet / we forget all that we have lived
    through / that hunger

that never stops for breath / Relief / would we call it that / What I
    am getting at / famished as I am
for life / my appetite barely whet / I can't believe I pass on
    chances and then regret
the last of days / There are other ways to starve yourself / retrieve
    your past when it's long spent /

Repent, repent / whisper to me your over-indulgence in all that's
    heaven sent /
we have lived through dark times and are hell-bent / the
    unfortunates lament
the stricken multitudes lighting up the way

Everybody Dies in Vain

Don't look back / flattering earth with the promise of itself / the
    torn cats are coming home
bedraggled, hurt and hungry / they're spraying pungent urine to
    mark their territory / this includes
you and me / waking from our muggy sleep / Me, a little boyish
    and embittered / you, flirtatious,

jittery from our love-making / it was not earth-shaking but
    brittle / our union urgent, unguent /
there is no calming ointment / Did we set out to save our skin,
    was that our fate / a chanced
confrontation, chantries sung and paid for / You were right, we
    were made for this / the swiftness

of the angels' fall / our celestial disgrace mistaken / a misplaced
    hawk gawking from the skies /
Try as we might we are no charter of disguise / exiled and
    feather-light we spite ourselves /
despoil what the ground defiles / everybody dies in vain / no one
    is ever satisfied

Do the Damned Thing Right

It is impossible to imagine the familiar maw of death / robbed of
    every cent / Despite the spill
of silver from our pockets / the moon, its light, the tree of heaven
    / I hate and fear myself /
The wretched end spiked like needle beer / the caw of crows
    reposing in white-feathered

dreams / it seems to me a haunting kind of summons / savage in
    the extremes / and I reject
the call / The paper skulls and clay / the sugar cane and corn,
    myrtle wreaths hung upon
the walls / the bathing in cold mountain streams / the railroad
    spur and engine trough

we happen on to quench our thirst / it's not enough / The beer is
    drunk in parks and slums
where desperate ones break rank / extend their wings / take flight
    / do the damned thing right /
The truth is quite indecent / distinguishes itself from the body /
    the crisis of thought /

Something is obviously wrong / the lonely absorptions are too
    hard wrought / the nightmares
that detest insomnia / the fevers, hives, boils and toothaches / the
    constant betrayals
lonesome and sought after / the blackmails and solicitations / the
    dull obscenity of prowled affection /

All this and more / cataracts, arthritis, heart disease / sickness,
    failure, our own private anguish /
the theatre of the absurd / Don't let us talk like that / mindful as
    we are of the animal waiting

to devour us / its ravenous jaws / Don't say a word / we are about
to be / extinguished

The Ambiguous Endings

Neither self nor other / the young girl's corpse, the faecal matter /
    The corrupt in us flattered
by its admiration / the rank and vile / ants, scorpions,
    mosquitoes, bees / the abject repugnancy
of constructed meaning / make of this what you will / Me in my
    tightly buttoned print blouse

and neat cardigan / you in your splashy flowing dresses and
    flashy jewellery / smoking endlessly,
your shoe as an ashtray, your voice hoarse and ragged / lie next
    to me / until blanketed in senility
they carry you in an ambulance to a nursing home / Death,
    please leave us alone / Before your full

length mirror you practice your kisses / seductively embrace
    yourself in a provocative contredance /
a cotillion of flashing petticoats as your changing partners turn /
    the pages of your scrapbook fond
with dance cards and pressed orchids / racy and boy crazy / I fall
    for you / a mink coat, a diamond,

stocks and bonds as my inheritance / Those are the meanwhiles
    and if so's / I had no intention
of being here after I had spoken / liver, stomach, lungs and bones
    chintzed with cancer / playing cards
until time ran out / Let's talk about that / maybe not / In any
    case, it's hard to face

the face of one so recently deceased / the jump cuts breathlessly
    released / la nouvelle vague / the cheap
and gaudy casket / There are so many ways to misrepresent my
    aches and pains / make no mistake

the rapid change of scene has left me violent and obscene,
    forbidden / like black market babies

and unwed mothers / intent on being transfigured, self-abnegated
    / Wait, there are others /
ambiguous endings, in-betweens / the extreme close-up and
    comedic intent / the melancholia
of syntactic nuance / death, that endless didactic nuisance we can
    no longer do without

It is Done, My Love, It is Done

Us the culprits, horned and hirsute, our horsehair perukes /
    blackened-face mummers
coupling like lovers aghast / amidst the cartloads of men thrown
    into churchyard pits /
troupes of pace-eggers, tipteerers, galoshins, guisers /
    quacksalvers resuscitating the dead /

the clatter of the horses' hooves / the rattle of the wheels / the
    waltz and gallopade,
the tumble in the ring / Distemper, putrid water, pestilence
    anticipate the executioner /
doomed to expiate our crimes with our lives / I loved you once /
    Brute beasts cast into earth /

the effluvia of the rich seeping from convalescent wards / the
    ci-devant with their lost title
and privilege / the turnkeys rising from their beds / the hood
    drawn over my head / mothers
and chaperons having hooked an eider son with a good rent-roll /
    rouged of face and false

front-letted walk me to my death / the drums beaten, the tocsins
    rung / Dip your hankerchief
and pike point in the blood, sip the succour from your lips / it is
    done, my love, it is done /
Nenia's funerary lament already sung, the soothing voice / the
    worm that does not die /

With wedge and crowbar, dim ruin and clouds of dust the one
    long grave is dug / death
poured out in raging floods / the fusillade and grapeshot / the
    hard won trade of locks of hair /

pockets of puce, mules high-laden with crosses, handbarrows
    heaped with plunder /

brandy swallowed out of chalices / Is it no wonder old men sit in
    market places / while their children
scrape surgeon's lint and their wives make bandages / sausages,
    pork puddings, pastries, meat /
the sugar barrels in the street, coffee chests, soap, cinnamon and
    cloves / pale-faced grocers

embracing the betrothed / the doffed bonnet, the hair toil-wetted
    / the muskets and rushlights
laid to rest / a red-wool nightcap and black-shag spencer
carmagnole / this tannery of human skins
worth flaying for good washed leather / A saying about the
    weather / I forgot we dare not speak

The Commotion of My Passing

I wait my turn on clumps of hay / the mounting pile of
   amputated limbs / surgeons in blood and pus-
stained coats working by candlelight / whiskey, quinine, slops,
   manure, offal, gangrene / the filthy
lucre of life's theatre / anesthetised and raving like Broadway
   critics / let's not nit-pick / the blurb ways

of someone else's days / the pin scratches, splinter pricks,
   pustulas, and abrasions that bring the curtain
down / chumps, the lot / Alright then, so the condemned man is
   electrified / cod-fried and he's had his
greasy chips / by God the bloodied limbs are five foot high / the
   saws and knives are out for us / I say

bring on the dancing girls, the chorus line / in any case there's
   more of us with gross atomic secrets
we're taking to the grave / I ask you, why save the best till last /
   the cast is overcast / don't blab too
much / keep troubles to yourself / I'm feeling fine / a healing of
   first intention / Don't mention it / okay,

okay, I'm sick . . . / a second class intervention / lunch then /
   cheese, crackers, tuna fish / how can I get out
of this / meanwhile all around us the war goes on / the covered
   carts and litters remove the wounded
from the field of battle / or transport the invalids in a retrograde
   march / my oh my, how we do prattle

on / perhaps another one of your songs / *here we go looby loo* /
   that moan, they say, was for your leg /
thrown on the rotting heap / let no one say the end comes cheap /
   not a peep / tomorrow

the packing and tentative goodbyes / and that's about the size of
  it / the rest and then some sleep /

the incredulous human vision of something better than that
  which is / all in stitches with thread
moistened by saliva / surgical knives sharpened on the soles of
  your boot / cornmeal and hardtack
fried in pork grease / arteries clamped and tied with silk / isn't
  that the truth / a fetid bayou

filled with floating cats / hands, arms, legs and feet / no way to
  sneak out on this / accept my kiss
without emotion / it's all the rage / And in the commotion of my
  passing . . . / *but you said* . . . / what
did I say / how did I set the stage / I am on my way out now /
  with nowhere left to go

Into the Dark and Out of Sight

Into this wild abyss of safe anchorage, bearing Italian wine,
     garum and metal ingots from god-knows-where / a bright sea
 flowing with jasper and liquid pearl / sailing into exile from such
     despair / an adulterer having plotted
my own father's overthrow / Just what is it that I know / From
     out of the inflamed night,

I charge the undertow and reach the spicy shore / wasted by
     angels, I lift my bow towards the rubber-burning
fires on the beach / the high tides switch to low / the shore-based
     winches turn / the cargo shifts / the ship
sinks, upright and intact / This is a fact / the garment factories,
     rail yards, oil rigs / drug-

barons and laundered cash have brought us to our knees /
     imposthumes, tick borne fever, malformed brains,
and killer bees / would I were wifeless or had childless died /
     Aside from that, they mean no harm / the summer
winds whip up a storm / and from the plumes of swirling dust /
     the acrid fumes of burning

paint and fuel / the excrement / Like locusts in a pitchy cloud, the
     workers swarm from wooden shacks behind
the dunes on heaving tracks / plastic sandals on their feet,
     oxygen canisters on their backs / their
mouths' stained red from chewing betal nuts / They wade into
     the muddied sand / chant,

and with bloodied hands hoist plates of steel upon their
     shoulders / cushioned with their safa scarves / I spill
my guts / this colony of makeshift huts rife with injury and
     disease / broken ankles, severed fingers,

smashed skulls, malaria, cholera, and dysentery / the sea foul
    with asbestos, oil, toxins, sludge, human

waste / Refrained from haste, they hack a coconut, and making
    up for what they lack, offer prayers for
their protection / the elephant god to watch their back / a goad, a
    noose, a broken tusk, a rosary, and laddoo /
a snake lassoed around the waist / the customary tattoo as the
    dismantling begins /

Crude hammers, axes, acetylene take the ships apart / slashed,
    burned, hacked down to the keel / from bow
to aft / the darkness and suffocating heat / grease and sludge / air
    thick with asbestos dust / the choking
smoke that billows on the brink of hell / where listless men worn
    out and beaten down

weld darker worlds / The sulphuric smell / backfires and
    flashbacks / toxic chromates in ballast-tanks / hull-plates,
boilers, copper-pipes / gaskets, pumps, flourescent lights / pulley
    blocks, steel ropes and shackles /
as the bulkheads are sliced and the deck-plate collapses / into the
    dark and out of sight /

The noises loud and ruinous / the heinous screams of humans
    plunging into endless flight / while
on their porches the scrap yard owners sip their sweet and milky
    tea, beyond reproach / In our
fall we stop and wonder / ponder the senseless nature of this long
    and distant voyage

Free Love

In this marriage of ours abusive and ill-conceived / I hide from
    everyone under the welfare motel bed / while
in the kitchen the fry cook sifts rat faeces from the flour / and
    hour by hour the bereaved give
birth to the underfed / the hippies already out to lunch serving
    free food over the counter-

culture / offering crash-pads for the homeless / tie-dyed shirts
    and whole wheat bread / this frame of reference
without cost / Beneath the mattress and springs melancholia
    comes creeping in / having
siphoned gas in the desolate all-night parking lot / junked cars
    and drunks refused at bars / the corpse

unfound for weeks on end / a magnum .44 beside it on the
    ground / unrecognisable even to his friends / But
all is not lost / we were made in another century were we not /
    asphalt, dust, dirt, and diesel fumes / rural rebels
giving hell / diggers, true levellers of real property / This life is
    mine / I know no poverty / there

are no boundaries, no enclosures / we're up-against-the-wall-
    motherfuckers armed with love / assassinating
poets with blanks / What's happening / my muse has other things
    for me to do / the beatniks, dropouts,
space-cadets are at the ranch / the hard-rock miners have given
    up the ghost / dodging

the draft and making dope-runs through the snow / the one-lane
    twisted road hugging the granite cliff / the rock-
strewn river below / Leaving nothing to chance / we're digging
    irrigation ditches, terracing gardens,

harvesting plants for dinner / our inner energy precariously
    balanced on this lofty ridge /

we aspire to deer antlers, the jawbone of an ass, nails, and
    bailing wire / perspiring in the sweat lodge, we chant
and rub cornmeal onto each other's burning bodies / then gorge
    ourselves on roasted goat, drink
homemade wine, smoke dope, make love with someone else's
    mate

the hobo bundles still hold out hope / their charms keeping in
    their arms the daughters of Albion
looking to the west / where women work on trucks, hold rifles
    and wield a pretty chainsaw
like Essenes men renouncing sex / annihilating themselves with
    the as yet unborn / the scorn

of cross-dressing celibates distributing birth-control / the
    nakedness of sin and shame / stricken
with remorse the holy beggars denounce the purse / camaraderie
    amoureuse / Oh Death,
you have refused my non-conformist caresses / and so, we'll
    rename Lucifer, the morning star,

as Venus / declare this marriage open, lewd, lascivious, and
    obscene / but no matter how much
I wash my hands of you, I can never get them clean / Beneath the
    bed the air is stifling / and the space
they claim is infinite and unending, is trifling, heart rending, and
    claustrophobic in the extreme

'Nobody is ever missing.'
—JOHN BERRYMAN, *Dream Song 29*

Notes

Songs

'The Song of the Dead-Child Being': Dead-Child Being – a child who died before it was baptised and was therefore not permitted to be buried in the graveyard with its family.

'The Song of the Dead Christ': 'The ground cracks and the earth opens to the abyss' –Pascal: *Pensées*, 72

'The Song of the Dying': Based on *Aided Óenfhir Aífe* (*The Death of Aífe's Only Son*) a story from the Ulster Cycle of Irish mythology.

'The Song of the Blind Heretic Harper': Inspired by the memoirs of Arthur O'Neill (1734–1818). Words or short phrases are occasionally woven into the poem.

'The Song of the Bone-Grubber': Inspired by *Life in the London Streets or Struggles for Daily Bread* by Richard Rowe 1881.

'The Song of the Borachan': The borachán was the master of ceremonies at the rowdy and often lewd Irish wake games such as 'Hurry the Brogue' and 'Drawing the Ship Out of the Mud.'

Visions

'Vision of Quicksilver 1': I have used elements of this small section from *Quicksilver: A History of the Use, Lore and Effects of Mercury* By Richard M. Swiderski: 'Dover's critic Daniel Turner recognized what would happen if women swallowed quantities of crude mercury in the pursuit of comeliness: they scattered it on the ballroom floor behind them in a trail bearing laughable resemblance to shining jewels. Mercury actually would affect women the same way it affected men and animals, as a laxative.' This led to the lines, 'The perfumed East ingesting quicksilver/ in pursuit of comeliness. A laxative trail of bejeweled globules scattered/on the ballroom floor . . .'

'Vision of Quicksilver II': In a similar way, some lines were influenced from phrases in *Incidents of Travel in Greece, Turkey, Russia, and Poland, Vol. 1 of 2* . . . By John Lloyd Stephens: e.g. 'two pistols and a yataghan in his belt', roaring 'quarantino'.

'Vision of the Healer': The line 'Phantasms of thinking throblets mouldering like antiquated trash.' Is an amalgam of a few lines of hearsay quote in *Isis Unveiled, Volume I, Science*, by H. P. Blavatsky.

'Vision of the House of Ill-Repute': 'importunities of loathsome young debauchees' adapted from the line 'the importunities of a loathsome young debauchee' from the article 'The Voice of the Dram Shop' by William C. Conant included in *Demorest's Monthly Magazine*, Volume 22, Issues 2–11, p434.

'Two-headed barmaids with skeletal feet' is adapted from a description of a painting (in *From Hogarth to Rowlandson: Medicine in Art in Eighteenth-century Britain*) that refers to a 'two-headed barwoman' and later refers to 'skeletal feet'.

Meditations

'Take Me Out to the Lowlands': first portion inspired by article, 'The Hulks at Woolwich' (from *The Criminal Prisons of London, and Scenes of Prison Life, Issue 7* By Henry Mayhew, John Binny).

'You Won't Awake': certain phrases taken from *The Life of John Berryman* by John Haffenden.

'It is Done My Love, It is Done': the phrase, 'the doffed bonnet, the hair toil-wetted' is from *The French Revolution a History: The guillotine, Volume 3* by Thomas Carlyle.

Acknowledgements

I am grateful to the editors of the following magazines, where some of these poems first appeared:

Song of the Dead-Child Being – *The Yellow Nib*
Song of the Dead Christ – *Stony Thursday Anthology 2018*
Song of the Dying – *Crannog*
Song of the Blind Heretic Harper – *Poetry New Zealand*
Song of the Bean Chaointe – *Causeway/Cabhair*
Song of the Bone Grubber – *Magma* (London, England)
Song of the Daysbird – *Harvard Divinty Bulletin*
Song of the Resurrectionists – *Branch Magazine*
Song of the Borachan – *The Moth* (Ireland)

Vision of a Sudden Death – *Orbis*
Vision of Quicksilver – *Revival*
Vision of Death's Virtues – *The Rusty Toque*
Vision of the Fear of Death – *Harvard Divinity Bulletin*
Vision of Light and Shadow – *Ottawa Arts Review*
Vision of the Healer – *The Warwick Review*
Vision of the Journey to Hell – *The Moth* June 2013
Vision of the Future – *Angionish Review*
Vision of Rust – *Abridged*: Rust edition
Vision of the House of Dust – *Poetry Salzburg Review* (University of Salzburg Press, Austria)
Vision of the Danse Macabre – *The Poetry Bus* #4 (Ireland) print and audio CD
Vision of Time – *Poetry Salzburg Review* (University of Salzburg Press, Austria)
Vision of the Blind Beggar – *Arc*
Vision of the Dead Land – *Abridged* 13, 2014

Meditation #1 Take Me Out to the Lowgrounds – *Ecotone* (US)

Meditation #2 This the Day of Slaughter, – *Cyphers*, No. 73 2012

Meditation #3 The Hour is Upon Us – *Poetry New Zealand* – also, *The Malahat Review*, Fall 2012

Meditation #4 Beyond the Dead – *The Literary Review of Canada*

Meditation #5 You Won't Awake – *Grain*

Meditation #7 The Hook is Slung – *In/Words* (Carlton University)

Meditation #8 This After All is Life – *Grain*

Meditation #10 Working the Height – *Ninth Letter Arts and Literary Journal* (University of Illinois)

Meditation #11 Curtain Call – *Burning Bush 2* (Ireland)

Meditation #12 Nothing is the Matter – *The Baltimore Review*

Meditation #13 Something Rare – *Guernica Editions: Poet to Poet Anthology* (Canada).

Meditation #14 What I am Scared of Most is Nothing – *The Rusty Toque*

Meditation #15: Where Away? – *Verse Wisconsin* (online) Mask and Monologue

Meditation #16 Striving to Stay Alive – *Connotation Press* (US)

Meditation #17 Profuse With Darkness – *Inkspill* (London, England)

Meditation #18 Indulge in Dying – *Connotation Press* (US)

Meditation #18 Indulge in Dying – *Sand – Berlin's English Literary Journal*

Meditation #19 Everybody Dies in Vain – *The Stony Thursday*

Meditation #20 Do the Damned Right Thing – *Abridged*: Railroad edition

Meditation #21 The Ambiguous Endings – *Ninth Letter Arts and Literary Journal*

This book has been typeset by
SALT PUBLISHING LIMITED
using Sabon, a font designed by Jan Tschichold
for the D. Stempel AG, Linotype and Monotype Foundries.
It is manufactured using Holmen Book Cream 65gsm,
a Forest Stewardship Council™ certified paper from the
Hallsta Paper Mill in Sweden. It was printed and bound
by Clays Limited in Bungay, Suffolk, Great Britain.

CROMER
GREAT BRITAIN
MMXXIII